Going Lightly!

Terrific Tips To Lighten Your Daily Load.

Sharon Bowman

Bowperson Publishing Company
Glenbrook, Nevada

Praise for
Going Lightly!

@ @ @ @ @

"Straight from her heart to the heart of the matter – these are great big chocolate-covered tips to DE-stress your life. Enjoy!"

Marcia Jackson, President
Training Resources, NC

"Sharon's terrific tips to help create lightness and sunshine in our daily lives are written simply so that we can remember them easily. Her colorful writing style convinces us to take action now. After reading Sharon's book, I choose to be a Sunshine Person!"

Carol Neal, Program Coordinator
Los Rios Community College, CA

"Whoever said life has to be so difficult? Sharon gives us terrific tips to show us how 'undifficult' life can be. Acting on these tips gets us sound results in the ways we interact with the world around us. A must read!"

Carol Kivler , President
Kivler Communications, NJ

"Go lightly and explore Sharon's guidance into endless possibilities for less stress and many more daily smiles!"

Barbie Hoeffer, Owner
Traditional Arabians, CA

"Sharon's inspired thoughts remind us that if we all unpack our bags each night, we would awake in the morning with a big smile on our face – and make this world a brighter place for all whose lives we touch."

Charlene Meenan, Director
The Glenbrook Project, NV

Going Lightly!

Terrific Tips To Lighten Your Daily Load.

Sharon L. Bowman, M.A.

Published by: **Bowperson Publishing**
P.O. Box 564, Glenbrook, NV 89413
Phone: 775-749-5247 Fax: 775-749-1891

Cover and text layout by: **Ad Graphics, Inc.**
Tulsa, Oklahoma 800-368-6196

Printed in the United States of America.

ISBN: 0-9656851-6-0

For my best friend,
Jan Thurman,
a Sunshine Person
who lightens the lives
of everyone she meets.

Angels can fly because they take themselves lightly.

G.K. Chesterton

Contents

◎　　◎　　◎　　◎　　◎

Terrific Tip №1:

Going Lightly
is A
State Of Mind.

Terrific Tip #1:
Going Lightly Is
A State Of Mind.

@ @ @ @ @

The Sunshine People. You know who they are. You work with them, maybe even live with one. Certainly you have a friend or two like them. They are the folks who walk into a room and suddenly the room seems a little brighter. They bring a cheeriness to the group they're chatting with. If they do get ruffled, they recover their sense of perspective quickly. They look with kindness and humor at themselves and others.

Sunshine People make everyone else feel a little better just by their presence. The workplace is lighter and brighter with them around.

Of course, you also know the Raincloud People – the co-workers, customers, friends, or family members who are convinced that life is a disaster waiting to happen. They make huge mountains out of tiny molehills, live from thunderstorm to thunderstorm, and are eager to share their dire predictions – with YOU! If something bad happens, Raincloud People are the first to say: "I told you so."

And then there's you. You're probably a little bit of both. On good days you smile at everyone. On bad days you feel like a little rain cloud yourself. And some days you just say a quiet prayer that you'll make it to the end of the day alive and in one piece.

So how do the Sunshine People do it? How do they keep their cheery perspective when things around them are going to hell in a hand basket?

Sunshine People know that
going lightly begins in their mind,
not in the world around them.

They know that perspective has more to do with what's in their head than the situations they find themselves in.

Sunshine People know that going lightly through their workday is about making choices – choosing to think, feel, see, say, and do things a little differently from most of us. They know that the small, almost insignificant choices they make can add up to big changes over time. They know that peace is a choice. So are joy, health, humor, tolerance, compassion, love.

This book will help you
do what Sunshine People do –
go through your day
with a lighter body, mind, and spirit.

Nope, this book won't take away the situations that you struggle with everyday. Instead, it will give you ways to maintain a sense of perspective, of humor, even of peace as you journey through your day. You will feel lighter and brighter – and the folks around you will pick up the vibes. The joy is in the journey. Bon Voyage!

They say that time changes things,
but you actually have to
change them yourself.

Andy Warhol

Terrific Tip №2:

People
Who Go Lightly
Sign Up
With A Smile.

Terrific Tip #2:

People Who Go Lightly Sign Up With A Smile.

◎   ◎   ◎   ◎   ◎

Those darn Sunshine People! They do silly things that no normal person would do. Like write little notes to themselves. Or wear a clown-colored tie. Or laugh at their own dumb joke. Or smile in the morning mirror and watch themselves smile back.

**Sunshine People know that
the silly things that make them smile
also give them
an endorphin boost for the day.**

As you know, endorphins are your brain's pleasure chemicals – they cause the pleasant, euphoric feelings you associate with things you like to do.

Anything that puts a smile on your face in the morning is your endorphin cocktail – and what a delicious way to start your day!

Try this endorphin boost to give you a grin as you begin your daily journey:

Write yourself a little message on a scrap of paper or a post-it note: *"Today we're going lightly, my friend!"* Or the note might say: *"Are you alive? Awake? Breathing? Then SMILE!"* Or: *"Any day is a good day when you can get out of bed alive!"*

Sharon L. Bowman. M.A.

Stick your note someplace where you'll be likely to see it first thing in the morning: to your alarm clock, bedpost, nightstand, mirror. In the morning, when you spot it, read it out loud to yourself (if you can do that without waking anyone else up).

Silly? Of course! That's the point. It'll put a smile on your face before you would normally even think about smiling. And it'll remind you that going lightly is first about play – having fun doing something kind of goofy like writing a note to yourself.

You might even change the note periodically, greeting your future self with messages like: *"So glad to see you're awake and happy this beautiful morning!"* Or: *"You're going to really enjoy this day."* Or how about a song line: *"I've got you, babe!"* *"Here comes the sun!"* (Guess you can tell which generation the author is from!)

Go ahead and try it – your emotional right brain will love you for it, even if your analytical left brain thinks you're nuts!

Bonus Tip: Write a little note of humor for another family member or friend. Tape it to a bedroom or living room door, or tuck it away where the other person will find it later in the day – when he or she needs an endorphin boost! And while you're at it, tuck another note away for yourself – then smile when you find it!

> *If you want to win anything*
> *– a race, your self, your life –*
> *you have to go a little berserk.*
>
> George Sheehan

Terrific Tip Nº3:

People Who Go Lightly Are Full Of Hot Air.

Terrific Tip #3:
People Who Go Lightly Are Full Of Hot Air.

❋ ❋ ❋ ❋ ❋

Think of a hot air balloon. It lies flat on the ground until someone fills it with what? You get the prize – hot air of course! And as it expands, it begins to float – slowly, peacefully, until it rises in all its multi-colored beauty. Ah, I wax poetic, but you get my drift!

Sunshine People do the same thing. Okay, so they don't float up in the sky. But they have something that reminds them to feel peaceful for seconds, or minutes, or hours. And feeling peaceful is kind of like floating.

What they have is what you have. You've had it since birth. It goes wherever you go. You can't leave home without it. And it's full of hot air too.

Know what it is? Of course you do – your breath! Actually, it's the ACT of breathing.

Sunshine People know that breathing is the winning ticket to a more light-hearted day.

Don't believe the Sunshine People? Check it out for yourself. Here's what you do: Simply stop moving (or reading), stay completely still, and exhale through your mouth. Push out all that stale air by pulling in your abdomen.

Sharon L. Bowman. M.A.

Now take a slow deep breath through your nose. Feel your abdomen expand first, then feel your chest rise, and finally your shoulders lift. Good. Now do it one more time. Want to go for a third?

How do you feel? A little lightheaded maybe. You just flooded your body and brain with fresh oxygen which it isn't used to having. You may also feel warmer. And definitely, for at least the duration of the breathing, you may feel more relaxed – dare I say "peaceful?"

So begin your morning with a smile, and then take a few slow deep breaths. As your body gets used to the oxygen, it'll also get used to the momentary feeling of calm relaxation from breathing deeply.

Yes, the feelings will probably fade as you move into the routine of your day. But you can reclaim them anytime you want by simply stopping all movement and taking two or three deep breaths, keeping your mind focused on your breathing while doing it.

Then stretch, yawn, smile, and continue on with your day! Your body and mind will thank you for it!

I've got to keep breathing.
It'll be my worst mistake if I don't.

Sir Nathan Rothschild

Terrific Tip №4:

People Who Go Lightly Unpack For The Trip.

Terrific Tip #4:

People Who Go Lightly Unpack For The Trip.

◎   ◎   ◎   ◎   ◎

Sunshine People do things backwards. They let go instead of holding on. They think less is more. And they unpack for a trip.

Now that's probably not what you do when you get ready to travel. In fact, you've already packed for your daily trip to work. Regardless of whether you're a man or a woman, you probably have a briefcase, handbag, wallet, box, or shoulder bag stuffed with the "essentials" you need for your day.

What if you had to dump out your wallet, bag, or briefcase, and take only what you could fit inside a standard letter-sized envelope? Could you do it? What would you take? What is "essential" to you and what isn't?

Your briefcase or handbag is a metaphor for your mind (perish the thought!). Some of the ideas and beliefs you carry with you are essential in your daily life. Others aren't. Some mental stuff is just clutter – old ideas and scripts that play over and over like long playing records (remember records?).

***In order to go a little more lightly,
Sunshine People let go of the mental clutter
and take only the essentials with them.***

Sharon L. Bowman. M.A.

How do you do that? First you have to be aware of the clutter. In the morning, after you've smiled at yourself and taken a few deep breaths, quietly empty your mind for a moment, letting all the cluttered thoughts fall onto a mental table.

You might notice the "raincloud" thoughts first, ones like: *"Too much to do and no time to do it,"* or *"If I don't hit the ground running, I'll be late for work."* Leave these thoughts on your mental table and sift through the clutter until you find one or two ideas that are absolutely essential to you. These are the thoughts or beliefs that, if you didn't have them, you'd feel as if your life wouldn't be worth living.

"Essentials" might be your belief in a Higher Power, the love of your family and friends, the knowledge that, in spite of what gets done or doesn't get done today, you're still a good person. An "essential" might be knowing that loving yourself is more important than being perfect. An "essential" might be knowing that the journey is only worth it if there is joy in it – and today you're going to find the joy. Or it might simply be that you're alive today (well, consider the alternative!).

Whatever your "essentials" are, take a moment to enjoy them – and take them with you when you walk out the door.

> *I keep the telephone of my mind*
> *open to peace, harmony, health,*
> *love and abundance.*
> *Then, whenever doubt, anxiety*
> *or fear try to call me,*
> *they keep getting a busy signal –*
> *and soon they'll forget my number.*
>
> Edith Armstrong

Terrific Tip №5:

People Who Go Lightly Take Only The Good Stuff.

Terrific Tip #5:

People Who Go Lightly Take Only The Good Stuff.

❀ ❀ ❀ ❀ ❀

Your analytical left brain is a busybody and a worrywart. It makes lists of things for you to do that you couldn't possibly get all done in a day. It scrutinizes your performance (and everyone else's too). It judges everything it notices, using words like: *"That's good, bad, right, wrong. You should or shouldn't. You'll never get it all done. You'll never get it perfect. I can't believe you did that – how embarrassing!"*

The left brain uses up a great deal of your energy that you could spend feeling more at ease with your life, if only you could find a way to stop its incessant analysis.

Sunshine People stop the left brain chatter
by choosing to think about things
that make them feel good instead.

You can make that choice too. Anytime you notice your left brain criticizing you or others, simply replace that thought with one that makes you feel good.

Things that make you feel good can be small creature comforts: a warm bed, a hot shower, colorful flowers, strong coffee. Or they may be work-related: the co-worker who always greets you with a smile, the gratification for a job well-done, the money you earn which buys you the things you enjoy. Or they may be of a more spiritual nature: gratitude for family and friends, guidance, health, grace, love.

No, you're not ignoring the negative stuff. You're not pretending that life is a bed of roses. You're simply reminding yourself that there's a lot to like about living, even when the dissatisfied left brain thinks there isn't.

By the way, people who go lightly DON'T begin their day by listening to the daily news. Later, maybe, but NOT first thing in the morning.

If you're a morning news person, you might protest, *"But I won't know what's going on in the world!"* Rest assured that the Raincloud People you know will be happy to share all the bad tidings with you!

Remember those Sunshine People? They take only the good stuff with them to work!

Bonus Tip: In addition to your morning smile, deep breathing, and choosing an "essential" to take with you on your daily journey, you can also make a quick "Attitude of Gratitude List" in your mind. While showering or sipping coffee, remind yourself of five (or ten or fifteen) things you're grateful for. Not profound stuff, just the things that make you happy, the things that you say a mental "thank you" for whenever you think about them.

> *Got no checks, got no banks –*
> *still I'd like to express my thanks.*
> *I got the sun in the mornin'*
> *and the moon at night.*
>
> Irving Berlin

Terrific Tip №6:

People Who Go Lightly Move About When in Doubt.

Terrific Tip #6:

People Who Go Lightly
Move About When In Doubt.

◎   ◎   ◎   ◎   ◎

So what makes the daily load feel heavy to you? Too much to do? Schedule interruptions? Health problems? People? Projects? Traffic? Noise?

Can't get rid of the things that make you feel physically and mentally uptight? Then DO something to change the physical and mental tension you feel.

**Sunshine People do it all the time –
when they begin to tense up,
and they don't know what else to do,
they MOVE.**

You can do it too. It doesn't mean you relocate to another job, house, or town. It DOES mean that you stand and stretch. Go get a drink of water. Wiggle your fingers and toes. Scrunch up your face. Raise your arms to the sky and then bend over and let them dangle in front of you. Shake out your hands. Lean backwards. Walk, skip, run (for even a short distance – like down the hall!).

When you begin to feel tense, your brain is sending messengers (stress hormones) to the rest of your body telling it to get ready to defend itself against whatever it is that's making you upset. The messengers give you extra physical strength to take care of the problem.

But if you don't use that extra hormonal "muscle," it just hangs out in your body for awhile, giving you the jitters and muddying up your thoughts. Let those stress hormones stick around inside your body everyday, and they'll eventually make you sick.

To dissipate them, you need to use them up. And to do that, you need to move. Oh, nothing like running a marathon or climbing a mountain. Simple movements like walking, bending, and stretching will do fine.

If you're at work, take a short hike to the restroom (where you'll do some deep breathing). Get outside for a bit. Do ten laps around your desk. Stand and stretch. Drop a pencil and pick it up – then do it again.

ANY movement will use up the stress hormones and get you back on track. You'll feel calmer and healthier, even if the tension-filled situation is still there. And sometimes you can think more clearly of a solution because you've given your mind, body, and spirit a mini-break from it all.

Bonus Tip: Build a "movement break" into every hour you work, especially if you have a desk-job or are on a computer a lot. Even 60 seconds of stretching will feel like a miracle to your cramped body – and its gratitude will be boundless!

> *My grandmother started walking*
> *five miles a day when she was sixty.*
> *She's ninety-five now,*
> *and we don't know where the hell she is.*
>
> Ellen Degeneria

Terrific Tip №7:

People Who Go Lightly Check Their Ticket Often.

Terrific Tip #7:

People Who Go Lightly Check Their Ticket Often.

◎   ◎   ◎   ◎   ◎

Remember what the winning ticket to a more light-hearted day is? If you need a hint, check Tip #3. If you said "breathing," you rang the bell!

**Sunshine People know that
they can't breathe deeply
and feel upset at the same time.**

It's a physiological impossibility.

When you're upset, your breathing becomes shallow and rapid, and your whole body tenses up. When you consciously take a few slow, deep breaths, the muscles in your body get more oxygen and your body relaxes. That's kinda nice to know when you're having a bad hair day.

Of course, the trick is to remember to stop whatever you're doing and spend a minute or so breathing slowly and deeply.

**Sunshine People "check their ticket"
(remember to breathe)
because they carry a reminder with them.**

They tie a small piece of colored ribbon, yarn, or tape to their watch, wrist, finger, or buttonhole. Or they tape a post-it note that says "breathe" where they see it of-ten. Or they set a stop-watch or timer to ring at certain intervals.

Whatever reminder they choose to use, they stop and breathe slowly and deeply whenever they see or hear the reminder.

A little odd having a bit of ribbon wound around your watch? Or a pipe cleaner scrunched up and stuck in your buttonhole? Yup. But by reminding yourself to stop and breathe at different times throughout your day – and focusing your mind on your breathing while doing it – you've created a few moments of physical peace and relaxation for your grateful body.

Interestingly enough, after awhile you won't even need the reminder. Your body will like the feeling so much that it'll remember on its own to stop and take a few deep breaths.

Bonus Tip: When a family member, co-worker, friend, or client asks you about your "reminder" – *"What IS that thing dangling from your wrist anyway?"* – use this "teachable moment" to show your friend how to take a few slow, deep breaths. And be sure to tell her how much happier and healthier she'll feel – just like you!

> ### How beautiful it is to do nothing –
> ### and then rest afterward.
>
> Spanish Proverb

Terrific Tip № 8:

People Who Go Lightly Reframe The Picture.

Terrific Tip #8:

People Who Go Lightly Reframe The Picture.

◎   ◎   ◎   ◎   ◎

Sunshine People make up lots of stories about the folks they meet – especially those people who do stupid or dangerous things.

You know who they are: the driver who suddenly cuts in front of you, the guy dashing down a crowded side-walk – and right into you, the kids playing carelessly in the middle of the street, the gal who zips into the park-ing space you were waiting for.

Let's take the reckless driver who cuts in front of you. What's your first reaction? Yes, you'd probably get a bit upset. Road rage? Not you!

What if you knew that the driver had a sick kid in the car and was rushing to the hospital? Would it change your reaction, at least a little? Probably.

Sure, it's a story. It's not even true. And it doesn't change the situation any. What it does is this: It changes your emotional reaction to the situation. And THAT changes your physical health and mental peace-of-mind.

**Sunshine People know that
the body can't tell the difference
between what is real and what isn't.**

Sharon L. Bowman. M.A.

It's not what's happening that's upsetting them. It's the picture inside their head – the interpretation of the situation – that makes them upset. So they simply change the interpretation of that picture – "reframe it" – so that their reaction to it is more positive.

Reframing the picture might sound like: *"That person is going through some awful family problems right now."* Or: *"She looks like she's feeling really down."* Or: *"He must have a lot on his mind to make him not pay attention."* Whatever the story is, it takes the sting out of the situation and makes it easier to handle.

To stay calm, Sunshine People
think the best of others, instead of the worst,
and they don't take anything personally.

Yes, people who go lightly DO stick up for themselves. And they DO hold others accountable for the consequences of their actions. They DON'T assume that the other person is incredibly stupid. And they DON'T assume that the other person did the dumb thing out of a personal vendetta.

Try it the next time you get upset at someone. Make up a story about the person. Cut him or her a little slack *("I've had days like that too.")* Reframe what's happening by imagining reasons for it other than what's obvious. And then handle the situation the way you feel is best.

What you're really doing is lightening your load by lightening your mind – and your body goes right along for the ride!

One way to get high blood pressure
is to go mountain climbing over molehills.

Earl Wilson

Terrific Tip №9:

People Who Go Lightly Play The Great Give Away Game.

Terrific Tip #9:

People Who Go Lightly Play The Great Give Away Game.

◎　◎　◎　◎　◎

Sunshine People play games. Children's games. Adult games. Doesn't make any difference what kind of game it is as long as it feels good.

One game they play that's especially helpful in lightening their load is the Great Give Away Game. You probably know it by its other name: Spring Cleaning.

Spring Cleaning isn't just about the spring, and it isn't just about the material things around you. The game can be played anytime, anyplace, and on any level – physically, mentally, emotionally, spiritually.

Sunshine People know that it takes energy to maintain stuff.

They know that all the stuff they hold onto – material things, sad memories, outdated beliefs, habitual emotional reactions – drain their time and energy. So they play The Great Give Away Game to reclaim all that lost time and energy.

The Great Give Away Game means you give, loan or sell things to others who may be able to use them. It means you toss, trash, or eliminate things you no longer need or use. It represents letting go of old mental patterns, beliefs, or emotions that no longer serve you or feed your soul.

The rules of the game are simple:

◆ Start small, with one item, one drawer, one closet, one thought pattern, one belief, one emotion.

◆ Begin in your mind first, mentally releasing the thing, idea or emotion and letting it go with relief and gratitude. Picture the space clean, organized, empty. Picture the idea or emotion floating away like a cloud in a summer's breeze.

◆ Physically do something to represent what you have mentally given away. Clean out that drawer, that file, that shelf. Write the thought or belief on a piece of paper and trash or burn it. Make a goodwill bag of stuff and drop it off on your next trip to town. Set a time limit so that, at the end of 15 minutes, 30 minutes or an hour, you stop, look at what you've done, and congratulate yourself on your accomplishment.

◆ If you find yourself thinking about the item or thought, or feeling the emotion, simply remind yourself that you gave it away. Then mentally let go of it again and choose instead to focus your mental energy on something that makes you feel good.

◆ The items you give away represent a reclaiming of space and energy for you. You'll actually feel lighter as you look at the empty closet, drawer, desk, office, or storage space around you. You'll feel lighter when you remind yourself that you gave away that old worn-out mental script, that negative belief, that habitual emotion.

The human race has been playing
at children's games from the beginning,
which is a nuisance for the few people
who have grown up.

G.K. Chesterton

Terrific Tip №10:

People Who Go Lightly Shrink The Space To Shrink The Things.

Terrific Tip #10:

People Who Go Lightly Shrink The Space To Shrink The Things.

◎   ◎   ◎   ◎   ◎

Have you ever moved from a small house to a bigger one? How about from a tiny office to a large one? Maybe you replaced your small, one-drawer desk with a cubby-filled roll-top. Or perhaps you added some storage space to a spare bedroom or garage.

If you've done anything like that, you probably noticed that quite soon all the shiny new space filled up just as tightly as before. In fact, you probably eyeballed it and thought, "Gee, it looked so big before I moved every-thing in and now I need to find more places to put things."

Sunshine People know that objects expand to fill the space available.

They also know that they really use only about 20% of what they own – the rest is there as backup, or for special occasions, or for sentimental reasons, or be-cause they can't shake the *"But I might need it someday"* thinking.

Now you don't have to empty out your house, office, or desk. And for pete's sake, don't stress yourself out by thinking of all the cleaning and clearing out that you

Sharon L. Bowman. M.A.

don't have time to do. Just do what folks who go lightly do: Play two little games with yourself.

First, play The Great Give Away Game (see Tip #9). Set yourself a goal. For example, by a certain day, you will give away at least 25% (maybe more, maybe less) of the things piled up in a certain closet, on one bookshelf, in a drawer, or in part of the garage.

Second, pretend that you don't have as much space as you really do. Look at your desk, bookshelf, closet, or garage. Mentally shrink that space to three-quarters (or one-half) of what it really is. Now see if you can eliminate enough stuff so that you actually have some empty space staring back at you. Amazing, huh?

Bonus Tip: Become aware of your own patterns of keeping, collecting, and hoarding. Casually look around and make a mental note of the things you no longer need, or haven't used for a millennium or two. Smile to yourself as you realize that your stuff has indeed expanded until it fills the space available.

Why the smile? Because you know that owning stuff means you're prosperous. Owning stuff is a sign that you'll always have whatever it is that you need. And it means that you can let go of some or all of it because you'll always have the means to get some more of it when you need or want it.

Notice To Our Guests:
If there is anything you need and don't see,
please let us know and we will show you
how to do without it.

Mary Fadden

Terrific Tip 11:

People Who Go Lightly Shorten The Time To Shorten The Work.

Terrific Tip 11:
People Who Go Lightly Shorten The Time To Shorten The Work.

⊚   ⊚   ⊚   ⊚   ⊚

Have you ever spent a whole day on a work-related task? Or maybe on a chore at home like housecleaning or painting? Maybe you spent the day doing it because you had that much time available.

Did you ever have to cut that time in half because something unexpected came up? Like a rushed deadline or unexpected company? Did you still complete the project or chore? Maybe you surprised yourself and got a lot more done in the shorter time than you thought you could.

Sunshine People know that work expands to fill the time available.

Just like shrinking the space to shrink the things, Sunshine People give themselves an imaginary deadline to get the work done in a shorter amount of time.

Play another little game with yourself. Take one task at work or one chore at home. Estimate how long you think it'll take you to get it done. Now cut that time down to two-thirds. Do the work with the shorter deadline in mind. When the time is up, check out how much you've accomplished. Maybe you haven't finished the work, but you probably got more done than you thought you would.

Sharon L. Bowman. M.A.

Another way to shorten the work is to ask yourself these questions: *"Which tasks can I give away, delegate, hand over, or let go of? Which tasks will soon become problematic if I don't do them now? Which tasks give me the greatest pleasure (or sense of relief) once I've done them? Which tasks, if left alone, WILL go away?"*

Think home as well as work. Think delegating to family members as well as to co-workers.

Of course, you must also let go of the need to have the job done perfectly (which is often harder to let go of than the job itself).

So shorten the time to shorten the work – and see what happens!

Bonus Tip: If an undesirable, work-related task can't be delegated, play the Great Give Away Game with your negative attitude about the task. Combine an unavoidable task with something that gives you pleasure, like music, mental planning, happy thoughts, or just the *"doing it for its own sake"* feeling of accomplishment. Reward yourself after you've done the work with something that makes you feel good. Choose to find some positive aspect about the job and focus your mental energy on that.

> ***I like work; it fascinates me.***
> ***I can sit and look at it for hours.***
>
> Jerome K. Jerome

Terrific Tip №12:

People Who Go Lightly Refill Their Own Pitcher.

FILL ME

Terrific Tip #12:

People Who Go Lightly Refill Their Own Pitcher.

◎　　◎　　◎　　◎　　◎

Y ou've heard the story many times and many versions:

"It had been a long, hot day and workers were tired and thirsty. The boss took a pitcher of water and began filling the workers' water glasses. Soon the pitcher was empty but the boss continued to pour nothing into empty glasses. Finally, a worker spoke up: 'Excuse me, but your pitcher is empty. You need to refill it first before you fill our glasses.' The boss looked at him and smiled. 'You're absolutely right.' She then left to refill her pitcher."

**Sunshine People know that
in order to serve others
they must serve themselves first.**

In order to have the health, time, and energy to help their co-workers, family, and friends, they must first take care of their own physical, mental, and emotional needs.

The following is a paraphrased excerpt from the fabulous (of course!) book **Shake, Rattle and Roll:**

"So what refills your pitcher? What are the small daily things that give you a lift, that replenish your energy when it's low, that make you smile and feel lighter? What keeps

your energy moving and flowing so that you can fill the water glasses of your family, friends, co-workers and customers without depleting your own? What do you do to renew and re-energize yourself?"

"Maybe a walk, a nap, or some hot tub time is in order. A change of pace or escape into a novel or a movie. Maybe something as simple as listening to your favorite music, dinner with friends or family, playing with kids (yours or the neighbors), or dancing. Perhaps a quiet chat with your significant other or a close friend, or a few moments of solitude while you listen to the sounds of silence (a luxury in our noise-filled culture)."

"If the truth be told, it's often easier to take care of others – your family, friends, co-workers, clients – than it is to take care of yourself. And in all the hustle and bustle of your daily work, it's often the norm to forget to nurture your own body and mind. You convince yourself that your crazy schedule is okay, you have to do it this way, and that you'll take a vacation after all the work gets done and when you have some spare time."

So, because you really matter, promise yourself that you'll go a little more lightly – and take better care of yourself. It's only when you refill your own pitcher that you can then serve your family, friends, co-workers, and customers in the ways you wish to help them.

> **The last time I saw him,**
> **he was walking down Lover's Lane**
> **holding his own hand.**
>
> Fred Allen

Terrific Tip №13:

People Who Go Lightly Take Themselves Lightly.

Terrific Tip #13:

People Who Go Lightly Take Themselves Lightly.

❀   ❀   ❀   ❀   ❀

Remember the Raincloud People? Everyday ups and downs become life and death experiences to them. Living is a very serious matter, fraught with dangers looming at every turn.

On the other hand, Sunshine People know that their life is only one tiny sparkle – a very precious one to be sure – in a very big universe. They don't ignore the daily ups and downs. They just remind themselves that, in the larger scheme of things, the events that fill their workday are often not all that important.

In order to take themselves lightly,
Sunshine People ask themselves
The Ten Year Question.

What's The Ten Year Question? *"In ten years, will this really matter to me?"* Or: *"In ten years, will I feel the same way about this?"* Or: *"In ten years, will I even remember this?"*

Asking yourself The Ten Year Question helps you eyeball situations with more perspective. It helps you lighten up on yourself and on those around you. It helps you let go of the need to be perfect (if that's one of the burdens you carry around everyday). It gives you a bit of

---

Sharon L. Bowman. M.A.

mental clarity as you remind yourself of what is "essential" in your life (see Tip #4).

When you step back and get a sense of perspective, the everyday hustle and bustle doesn't seem quite as serious as before. You smile more, laugh more, and feel lighter about it all.

Bonus Tip: To really take yourself lightly, you need to quiet your critical left brain. Give it a job to do (like counting something, anything), then do Tip #5 again. Or go for something silly, like Tip #2. Or play The Great Give Away Game (Tip #9) and give away your self-judgment. Wonderful how light the load feels with that gone!

Don't take yourself too seriously.
And don't be too serious
about not taking yourself too seriously.

Howard Ogden

Terrific Tip №14:

People Who Go Lightly Savor The Souvenirs.

TREASURES FROM THE TRIP

JOY

LOVE

HUMOR PEACE

Terrific Tip #14:

People Who Go Lightly Savor The Souvenirs.

◎   ◎   ◎   ◎   ◎

You know what it's like to come home from a vacation with a pocket, bag, or box full of souvenirs. The odd-shaped rock you stumbled over, the delicate sea shell, a postcard, trinket, book, or photo. Maybe a piece of artwork or gifts for family and friends.

You also have a mind full of vacation stories – some of them amusing, surprising, or dramatic. All of them memorable.

Everything that happens on a vacation becomes part of the story-telling. As time goes by, even the upsetting things that may have happened (the cancelled flight, the horrendous storm, the screaming kids, the bug-infested cabin) are added to the stories as funny or suspenseful chapters.

Your daily journey to work is also a part of your very personal story. The ups and downs you experience each day become bits and pieces of the chapters you create as you live your story. And, given time, the down times are every bit as precious as the up times.

Sunshine People know that
each moment is a souvenir to be treasured.

It all becomes a part of who you are. The glad times, mad times, sad times, and bad times are what make you uniquely you. And they bring you unexpected gifts for the future – wisdom, compassion, humor, tolerance, hope, healing, love.

So savor your daily journey and every moment it contains. No one else's journey is exactly like yours. Your stories are a one-time only creation. The souvenirs you collect are unique and priceless.

In the evening, before going to bed, take a moment to tumble the souvenirs out of your mind and onto the mental table where you did your morning sorting of what's "essential" (remember Tip #4?).

This time think back briefly over your day, noticing what you experienced and how you felt about each thing that happened. Then gently scoop all the memories into a mental basket or box. If you want to hold one or two of the very best souvenirs in your mind for awhile, go ahead. Or you may want to weave the moments into a personal story for that day.

When you're ready to let go of the day, close the box, put a lid on the basket, and put it on a mental shelf with gratitude. The day is over, the souvenirs treasured and stored, the stories told, and you can go to bed with a lighter spirit. Sleep with the angels who take themselves lightly!

> *Keep some souvenirs of your past,*
> *or how will you ever prove*
> *it wasn't all a dream?*
>
> Ashleigh Brilliant

Tip №15:

People Who Go Lightly Lighten The Way For Others.

Tip #15:

People Who Go Lightly Lighten The Way For Others.

@   @   @   @   @

The real gift that Sunshine People bring to this world is one of light. Because of the quirky way they look at things (head tilted to the side, humor shining out from their eyes), they don't get lost in a fog of fear. Instead, they smile and say: *"Yes, you could think of it that way. Or you could think of it this way instead."* And they give us another way of looking at a situation that is different, funny, thoughtful, healing.

Sunshine People don't pretend there aren't heartaches in their lives. And they have their down days just like the rest of us. But they do something that we often forget to do when the clouds roll in.

Sunshine People look for the silver lining inside the clouds.

They try to find the gift in the adversity, the blessing in the trial, the light in the darkness. And when they do that, they make our loads a little lighter too. We feel better for having known them and talked to them. We feel better for having looked at the world through their eyes, even for a minute.

So become a Sunshine Person! It's not as hard as you think – and you're already half-way there. On the days your journey is feeling good, you're shinin' like the sun and the folks around you bask in your warmth.

And on the days your journey takes you into the swirl of a sudden thunderstorm, use some of the tips in this little book to create a silver lining for yourself and those you care about.

Smile. Do something silly. Stop and take a deep breath whenever you can. Think about the "essential" things that make life worth living. Remind yourself of all the things you're grateful for. Move and stretch. Breathe some more. Reframe the picture. Play a game. Give something away. Shrink the space. Shorten the time. Refill your own pitcher. Take yourself lightly. Collect your souvenirs, tell your own story, and rest easy.

It's all about choices – YOUR choices. You can choose the clouds or you can choose the sun. Both are inside you. Neither has anything to do with what's around you.

Your world changes because of the choices you make. And as you choose light, peace, healing, joy, and love, your world begins to reflect those things, like water reflects the sunlight.

Folks around you feel the difference in you and begin to go more lightly too. Pretty soon you realize you're lightening the way for others – just like those cheery Sunshine People!

My cousin has great changes coming:
One day he'll wake up with wings.

"The Caterpillar Song"
Incredible String Band

The song is to the singer,
and comes back most to him.
The teaching is to the teacher,
and comes back most to him.
The love is to the lover,
and comes back most to him.
The gift is to the giver,
and comes back most to him.
It cannot fail.

Walt Whitman

There's night and day, brother,
both sweet things;
sun, moon, and stars, brother;
all sweet things.
There's likewise a wind
on the heath.
Life is very sweet, brother.

George Borrow

Sunshine on my shoulders
makes me happy.

John Denver

Sharon L. Bowman. M.A.

Bonus Tips To Get The Most From Going Lightly

◎   ◎   ◎   ◎   ◎

◆ **Copy the chapter title pages with the cartoons** (you have the author's permission to do this). Hang one up each week where you can see it often (the refrigerator at home, on a mirror in the bathroom, on the dashboard of your car, on a wall at work, on your computer). Change it so that you focus on a different one each week. Color the words and cartoons so that they capture your visual attention.

◆ **Copy and share the chapter title pages with friends** so that they can post them at home or work too. Better yet, gift your friends with copies of the book!

◆ **Choose a tip-of-the-week** to practice daily for one week. They don't have to be chosen in order. Put a silly, fun, or colorful sticker in your calendar book for each day that you remember to do that tip. Forgive yourself if you forget.

◆ **Use colorful pens to print or write your tip-of-the-week.** Jazz up the page with glitter, stickers – whatever fun craft items you like. Hang your hand-decorated page where you can see it daily. Make some for your friends.

◆ **Explain or demonstrate your tip-of-the-week** to a family member, friend, or colleague (this reinforces the learning and may help your friend go a bit more lightly too!)

◆ **Form a "Going Lightly Club"** with other friends. Use the book as your resource. Check in with each other weekly to see how it's going. Praise each other lavishly for the baby steps you take.

◆ **Keep a "Going Lightly Journal"** and write down the little things you do each day for yourself and for others – things that brighten and lighten your day.

◆ **Introduce a Raincloud friend to a Sunshine buddy.** Also, help your Raincloud friend "reframe the picture" when a situation feels stormy.

◆ **Recognize the part of yourself that is a "Raincloud Person"** and the part that is a "Sunshine Person." Be aware of which part is doing your thinking for you: "Oh, there's that Raincloud thought again!" Or: "Now I'm doing some Sunshine thinking!" No judgment – just awareness.

◆ **Hold a "Going Lightly Lunch"** once a month: Get together with family, friends, or colleagues and share your favorite Going Lightly Tip (one from the book or one you make up yourself).

◆ **Look for the Sunshine People you know** and thank them for lightening up your life!

◆ **Make up your own collection of Going Lightly Tips** and Sunshine People ideas – and write your own book!

A Personal Note
To You From Sharon

@   @   @   @   @

Richard Bach, in his book *Illusions,* says that:

We teach best what we most need to learn.

He also says:

Learning is finding out what you already know.
Doing is demonstrating that you know it.
Teaching is reminding others
that they know it just as well as you.
We are all learners, doers, and teachers.

I, like you, am still learning how to go lightly – day by day, step by step. As we learn, we teach. And as we teach, we learn.

We all want to make a difference, to somehow matter, to have a reason for living – and what better way to do that than to shine in our own unique way, with our own special light?

No matter what we are, no matter what we do, we are precious. We are cherished. It matters that we're here. AND – by being who we are, we CAN lighten the way for others while lightening our own daily load.

Email me (**Sharon@Bowperson.com**) or fax me (**775-749-1891**) with your own "going lightly" ideas and I'll post them on my web-site at **www.Bowperson.com.** That way we'll learn together while we teach each other how to be the best Sunshine People we can possibly be! Here's to us – and our own Going Lightly Journeys!

Sharon Bowman, Lake Tahoe, January 2003

About Sharon

@ @ @ @ @

S haron Bowman has been a professional speaker, author, teacher, and trainer for over thirty years. She works with people who want to fine-tune their information-delivery skills, and companies that want to offer exceptional in-house training programs.

She is a workforce development and Fortune 500 trainer as well as state and community college adjunct faculty member.

Sharon has written five other practical, how-to books on motivation, teaching, and training. She practices what she preaches and uses an interactive, hands-on approach to everything she teaches.

Sharon is also The Trainer's Coach. She works with teachers and trainers on a one-on-one basis to fine-tune existing programs and to create new ones – programs that are high-energy, fun, and memorable for all.

For more information about Sharon, her personal coaching services, her interactive keynote and conference sessions, and her public and in-house training programs, contact her at:

Sharon L. Bowman, M.A.
P.O. Box 564, Glenbrook, NV 89413
Phone: 775-749-5247 Fax: 775-749-1891
E-Mail: Sharon@Bowperson.com
Web-Site: www.Bowperson.com

About Sharon's Books

© © © © ©

Sharon's popular "how-to" books are used by teachers, trainers, public speakers, presenters, human resource staff, and parents all across the country. See the descriptions below, or log onto **www.Bowperson.com** for more information.

Shake, Rattle and Roll!

Toys, gadgets and gizmos, movement and metaphor. From simple, ordinary things, you can create extraordinary learning experiences for your students, audiences, and training participants. With *Shake, Rattle and Roll*, you'll discover over one hundred ways to make learning come alive with energy, excitement, meaning and memory.

ISBN 0-9656851-3-6 • $17.95

How To Give It So They Get It!

Explore the ways you learn, teach, train, and give information to others. With easy-to-follow instructions for forty experiential training activities, *How To Give It So They Get It* will have you soaring with fresh ideas and renewed enthusiasm for teaching anyone anything and making it stick!

ISBN 0-9656851-2-8 • $17.95

Presenting with Pizzazz!

This book gives you a host of easy-to-apply tips and activities for getting learners of all ages more actively involved in their own learning. Based on accelerated learning research and written in a fun, conversational style, *Presenting with Pizzazz* is a resource gem for today's busy teachers, trainers, and public speakers.

ISBN 0-9656851-0-1 • $14.95

ISBN 0-9656851-5-2 • $15.95

Preventing Death by Lecture!

You KNOW there's a better way to present information to your listeners than straight lecture. So WHAT do you do to involve your listeners without wasting time? HOW do you turn YOUR listeners into learners? If you want to make your lectures, presentations, speeches, and classes interactive and unforgettable, this book is for YOU!

If Lazarus Did It, So Can You!

This is the Christian ministry version of *Preventing Death by Lecture* – with extra tips written especially for ministers, teachers, and parents. Use these terrific tips to help resurrect the learning in your churches, school, and homes.

ISBN 0-9656851-4-4 • $17.95

ISBN 0-9656851-6-0 • $15.95

Going Lightly!

Discover quick, easy ways to make your day feel lighter and brighter! Give this gift of sunshine to friends and colleagues! Brighten the lives of your staff and customers with copies of *Going Lightly!* Quantity discounts are available at Bowperson Publishing.

You can special order Sharon's books from your local bookstore. You can also contact the following distributors: The Trainers Warehouse (800-299-3770), The Humor Project (518-587-8770), Creative Training Techniques (800-383-9210), or by calling Bowperson Publishing at 775-749-5247. You can also order online at: www.amazon.com, www.barnesandnoble.com, or www.borders.com.

Resources To Help You Go Lightly

@   @   @   @   @

Bless This Mess. Joanna Slan

Getting in Touch with Your Inner Bitch.
Elizabeth Hilts

Gifts from a Course in Miracles.
Editors: Frances Baughan and Roger Walsh

Illusions: The Adventures of a Reluctant Messiah.
Richard Bach

I'm Too Blessed to be Depressed. Joanna Slan

Life 101. John-Roger and Peter McWilliams

One Minute for Myself. Spencer Johnson

Pocket Massage for Stress Relief.
Clare Maxwell-Hudson

Repacking Your Bags. Richard Leider

Stress Breakers. Helene Lerner

Stress for Success. David Lewis

**The Artist's Way: A Spiritual Path to Higher
Consciousness.** Julia Cameron

The Complete Idiot's Guide to Managing Stress.
Jeff Davidson

Time Management for Unmanageable People.
Ann McGee-Cooper

Your Body Believes Every Word you Say.
Barbara Levine